The Beat
THE MUSIC SCENE

ANNE BURKE

Editorial Board

David Booth • Joan Green • Jack Booth

STECK-VAUGHN
Harcourt Achieve

www.HarcourtAchieve.com

10801 N. Mopac Expressway
Building # 3
Austin, TX 78759
1.800.531.5015

Steck-Vaughn is a trademark of Harcourt Achieve Inc. registered in the United States of America and/or other jurisdictions. All inquiries should be mailed to Harcourt Achieve Inc., P.O. Box 27010, Austin, TX 78755.

Rubicon © 2006 Rubicon Publishing Inc.
www.rubiconpublishing.com

All rights reserved. No part of this publication may be reproduced or transmitted in any form or by any means, electronic or mechanical, including photocopying, recording, taping, or any information storage and retrieval system, without permission in writing from the copyright owner.

Project Editors: Miriam Bardswich, Kim Koh
Editorial Assistant: Wafa Mohamad
Art/Creative Director: Jennifer Drew-Tremblay
Designer: Sarah Anderson, Gabriela Castillo

6 7 8 9 10   5 4 3 2 1

The Beat: The Music Scene
ISBN 1-41902-417-5

CONTENTS

4 Introduction

6 **Gimmicks that Rule the Music World**
From Michael Jackson's famous glove to Britney's infamous school uniform — a timeline capturing the gimmicks musicians use to become famous.

10 **Poetry of Gordon Downie and Jewel**
Didn't know that the lead singer of the Tragically Hip and Jewel both wrote poetry? Well, they do.

12 **Electric Guitar**
An article about one of the most popular instruments in musical history.

16 **Everyone Wants to be an Idol**
Millions of viewers (and voters!) tune in to *Idol* in more than 20 countries. Read about the *Idol* craze in this article.

20 **Creating a First-hit Wonder**
Ever dream of writing a song and watching it performed in front of 30 million people? Joel Parkes did, and this newspaper article tells the story.

22 **Daneisha and the DJ Crew**
A classic "Battle of the Bands" graphic story.

26 **How to Become a VJ**
Think you've got the personality and talent to be a VJ on MTV or MuchMusic? Check out this article on how to land the job.

30 **Sound Recording Technology**
You know about MP3s and iPods — but what the heck is a phonograph? This graphic chart sorts it all out for you.

32 **Down-low on Downloading: Gift or Theft?**
Read what Eminem, the Barenaked Ladies, and Anastacia say about downloading in this article.

34 **Record Companies: Heroes or Villains?**
Sure they make a lot of music, but they've also been known to make a lot of noise complaining about burning CDs.
An opinion piece on the industry.

36 **Before They Were Rock Stars**
How did they get to the top? What was their big break? Find out in this report.

40 **Fan Mania!**
Beatlemania, Deadheads — these fans just can't get enough.

42 **Guitar Dreams**
Nathan's goal is simple — get Johnny Revolution to sign the 1972 Galaxy guitar and sell it online. Check out how he gets more than he bargained for in this short story.

WHERE WORDS FAIL, MUSIC SPEAKS

— Hans Christian Andersen (1805–1875)

GIMMICKS
that Rule the Music World

warm up

"There is no such thing as bad publicity." Do you agree with this statement?

Fans often believe that a rock star's image is happenstance and natural. In fact, for many artists, their appearance and trademark moves are mostly carefully planned and created to attract attention. They are gimmicks designed to make them stand out from the pack. While musicians often invent their gimmicks themselves, savvy record companies and managers do a great job of creating many of these zany but compelling looks.

1970s & 80s

▼ KISS

The "Glam Rock" Years

The band **KISS** was transformed into huge stars by their mysterious, superhero makeup. They developed complete personas around their characters and were never photographed without their makeup. The band never considered removing their masks. While they were often criticized for the use of this gimmick to sell music, no one can argue with their success.

Metal bands such as **Twisted Sister** and **Mötley Crüe** used hair and makeup as gimmicks to sell themselves.

happenstance: *by chance*　　zany: *comically ridiculous*
personas: *personalities*

1980s

Theatrical Looks

Huge, crazy glasses were **Elton John's** trademark.
Michael Jackson fashioned a white glove as a part of his act.
Boy George wore dreadlocks and smocks for a "unisex" look.

▲ Elton John

1990s

Emergence of the Girl and Boy Bands

The **Spice Girls** auditioned for their roles from a newspaper ad. Each had a persona — Sporty, Baby, Ginger, Posh, and Scary — designed to appeal to a specific group.

Their song *Wannabe* was Number 1 in Great Britain, making them the first girl band in history to top the world charts. Their movie, *Spice World*, brought about the term "Girl Power."

The popularity of their music was seen as empowering for female teens, but it was obvious that the Spice Girls were capitalizing on the body image of females.

***NSYNC** & **Backstreet Boys**: Their gimmick was Broadway dancing with no instruments, inspired by the popular Jackson 5 and music videos.

Justin Timberlake of *NSYNC went on to become a very successful solo artist.

▲ Spice Girls

capitalizing: *profiting from*

There is no such thing as "bad publicity." What is important is the gimmick — it is a reason for the press to talk about artists and the public to remember them.

1990s

Fashion and Makeup Notoriety

Marilyn Manson is notorious for combining his horror makeup with aggressive music. He aims for shock value. Manson is continually changing his image through his videos; every decision he makes with regard to image is ultimately about selling records and sending messages. Rob Zombie also uses this kind of "grotesque" gimmick.

Biggest Contender in Fashion

Known as the "Material Girl," Madonna is said to be a chameleon as she changes her image for each album, creating new fashion trends along the way. She has always been controversial and has gained much media exposure as a result.

▲ Madonna

◀ Nirvana

The "No Gimmick" Gimmick

The early 1990s saw the emergence of the Seattle, Washington grunge bands. Pearl Jam led the way with their "anti-fashion" approach. The cheaper and more vintage the clothing, the better. Having no gimmick became the gimmick. The "alternative" movement also included bands such as Nirvana and Soundgarden.

vintage: *second-hand; characteristic of the era it's from*

2000s

▲ Nelly

▲ Avril Lavigne

Simple Fashion Gimmicks that Started a Craze

Britney Spears gained notoriety by wearing a school uniform in one of her videos.
Nelly sported a simple bandage on his left cheek in honor of his little brother.
Avril Lavigne started a craze by wearing her father's old neckties.
Jennifer Lopez turned casual sports wear into high fashion.

Controversy that Sells

Controversy generates publicity and there is a belief in the music business that there is no such thing as "bad publicity." What is important is the gimmick — it is a reason for the press to talk about the artist and the public to remember them.

In the 1970s and 1980s, rock stars flaunted images of overindulgence, including wild parties, flashy cars and clothes, and, for the men, beautiful women.

Some hip-hop artists brandish guns in their videos, suggesting "street cred." Stars like **Eminem** have deliberately written lyrics that offend other stars. Artists like **50 Cent** use sayings like "bling bling" that show attitude.

▲ Eminem

wrap up

1. Select one gimmick presented in the article and explain why you think it would appeal to fans.

2. Girl bands like the Spice Girls popularized the saying "Girl Power." Some music reviewers thought it was positive while others saw it as negative. Based on the article, explain your view.

3. Create a new image and gimmick for your favorite artist. This could be fashion, hair, or stage moves. "Sell" your gimmick to your classmates.

Toboggan Hill

warm up

These two poems were written by singers Gordon Downie and Jewel. Notice the similarities between poetry and song lyrics.

I'm thinking back to when we were young
and eating donuts
with a set of plastic vampire teeth
that we were passing back and forth.
We weren't so young as to
think a dog was a horse.
Nor were we old enough yet to name
the cold purpose of musical chairs.
We were like-minded spirits
eking out a rhythm
whispering transmissions
through wet woollen mittens.
Growing up on a toboggan hill
nothing was material.
I'm thinking back to when we were young
If only to find out
forensically
what it was
we used to
want.

— Gordon Downie

eking out: *trying to make something happen*
forensically: *after much examination*

▲ Gordon Downie

wrap up

1. Explain the meaning of the lines: *Nor were we old enough yet to name/the cold purpose of musical chairs.*

2. Toboggan Hill is a place that Gordon Downie remembers from his childhood. With a partner, discuss what this place means to Downie. Share memories of your favorite place with your friends.

Pretty

▲ Jewel

There is a pretty girl
on the
Face
of the magazine
And
all I can see
are my dirty
hands
turning the page

— Jewel

wrap up

1. Briefly explain how the idea of "*pretty girl/on the/Face/of the magazine*" contrasts with the lines: "*And/all I can see/are my dirty/hands/turning the page.*"

2. Share with your friends a story showing the power that rock stars have over teens and their self-image.

Electric

It took the genius of Leo Fender to create the first **truly electric** instrument.

warm up

If you were asked to learn a musical instrument, would you choose the guitar? Why or why not?

Rock Stars

It's hard to imagine rock and roll without the electric guitar. Almost every one of us has imagined ourselves standing onstage, a wall of amplifiers behind, slamming out power chords for a horde of screaming fans. Although fashions come and go in the music business, the electric guitar has remained the instrument of choice for **aspiring** rock stars all over the world.

aspiring: *hopeful*

Guitar

Fender Stratocaster

Fender Telecaster

FYI

Leo Fender, the creator of the Telecaster and the Stratocaster electric guitars, could not play a note.

He was inducted into both the Rock and Roll Hall of Fame and the Country Music Hall of Fame for his electric guitar designs.

Music Scene

Compared to many other musical instruments, the electric guitar is a relative baby. Its roots go back to the big band era of the 1920s and '30s. As bandleaders like Benny Goodman and Duke Ellington began creating huge horn sections and playing large halls, their rhythm guitar players found themselves lost in a sea of trumpets and saxophones. In order to be heard above the general racket, they began experimenting with placing cheap radio microphones inside or onto their guitars. Though the results were mixed, at least they and their audience could hear the guitars. These weren't really electric guitars — they were acoustic instruments with a microphone attached.

King of Swing

Duke of Jazz

---

acoustic: *not electrified*

Early Invention

It took the genius of Leo Fender to create the first truly electric guitar. Fender realized that if he could build a better pick-up, the acoustic properties of the acoustic guitar would not matter. As well, because his new guitars would be made out of solid wood, the shape didn't matter at all — he could make them any shape he liked. Fender built a magnetic coil pick-up, which ran on low voltage and easily plugged into the early amplifiers. In 1950, he combined this with a unique new guitar design, which he called the Telecaster. It was an instant hit. A few years later, he perfected the design with a guitar named the Stratocaster. Both models were embraced by guitar players, and still sell in huge quantities today.

embraced: *welcomed*

Fender's Design

Almost all electric guitars still follow Fender's basic design, though they are made from many different materials. Fender made his electric guitars out of solid wood, but today's manufacturers use plywood, plastic composites, and even Plexiglas. With the addition of ever-larger amplifiers and cheap electronic effects boxes, the player can create an infinite variety of sounds. The most popular sound for most beginners is perhaps the combination of the distortion box and an amplifier turned up full blast, resulting in the crunching hard rock sounds loved by punk and metal players everywhere.

infinite: *endless*

Jimi Hendrix was the most inventive rock guitarist of all time. He even played a right-handed Fender Stratocaster upside-down and left-handed.

"It was amazing to hear someone play so well ... and with the guitar backwards! ... Because all the strings and notes are reversed ... all the chords are reversed ... and instead of bending a string you'd have to pull it."
— Mick Taylor

"He didn't have a very good voice but made up for it with his guitar."
— Mick Jagger

inventive: *creative*

▲ Jimi Hendrix playing his backwards Stratocaster.

Rock stars like **_Eric Clapton_** helped to popularize certain makes of guitars. In June 1965, Eric Clapton bought a second-hand Gibson Les Paul cherry sunburst guitar. He created a new electric guitar sound with it, and the Gibson Les Paul became a popular item. Today, vintage Gibson Les Paul sunburst guitars from 1958–1960 are valuable collectors' items.

In 1967, Eric Clapton bought "Brownie," a 1956 Fender Stratocaster with a sunburst finish and maple neck. The guitar is featured on the album cover of Clapton's first solo album, *Eric Clapton* (1970). "Brownie" set a world record for the highest price ever paid for a publicly sold guitar when it was bought at an auction in 1999 for $497,500. The money was donated to a charity.

vintage: *of the earliest time and highest quality*

▲ Eric Clapton and his "Crash 3" Stratocaster designed by a famous street artist.

10 BEST ROCK RIFFS OF ALL TIME
(according to UltimateGuitar.com)

Nirvana	*Smells Like Teen Spirit*
Led Zeppelin	*Whole Lotta Love*
Deep Purple	*Smoke on the Water*
Eric Clapton	*Layla*
Jimi Hendrix	*Voodoo Chile*
Metallica	*Master of Puppets*
AC/DC	*Back in Black*
Black Sabbath	*Paranoid*
Rolling Stones	*Satisfaction*
Rage Against the Machine	*Killing in the Name of*

riffs: *catchy guitar lines*

wrap up

1. In a short paragraph, explain how bandleaders like Duke Ellington and Benny Goodman helped create the need for the early electric guitars.

2. Discuss why the electric guitar remains the most popular instrument in today's music scene.

3. Create a poster for a new electric guitar that you have designed. What would you include on your poster to get musicians to buy and use your new design?

Everyone Wants to be an Idol

Idol fans "camp out," waiting for auditions.

warm up

Have you ever been in a talent show like the *Idol*? What do you think it takes to audition for it?

CHECKPOINT

What is your opinion of the show's popularity?

The *Idol* show is big business and a worldwide phenomenon! Beginning as the *Pop Idol* television show in the United Kingdom, the *Idol* format has been extended to more than 20 countries worldwide.

Why are the *Idol* shows so wildly popular? Is it the shared dream of becoming a rock star? Is it the attraction of the media? Or is it the sheer entertainment of seeing the meek, untalented, and wild — humiliated in front of millions?

phenomenon: *remarkable event*

The judges of *American Idol* — (left to right) Simon Cowell, Paula Abdul, Randy Jackson.

Ryan Seacrest, host of *American Idol*, has become a celebrity.

CHECKPOINT
Do you agree that many contestants "have little real musical ability but plenty of determination"? Why?

In addition to the US and Canada, *Idol* has been broadcast in the UK, South Africa, Poland, Germany, Belgium, the Netherlands, Norway, the Pan-Arabic region, France, and Finland.

The 2004 *American Idol* started out with 70,000 contestants. Almost 31.5 million viewers watched the final show, and more than 75 million votes were cast to select the winner.

Winners of the *Idol* show from 11 countries competed in the *World Idol* competition in 2004. Kurt Nilsen from Norway was voted the winner.

Many viewers see themselves reflected in the contestants on television. They are able to empathize with the struggling contestants, many of whom have little real musical ability but plenty of determination. Moreover, the voting system gives viewers a unique control over the show's outcome. They are able to decide who becomes famous or who goes home defeated.

The producers of the show claim that it is all about the contestants. However, the hosts and judges also play a big part in keeping everyone watching. Like all reality shows, there is no script, so the personality and style of the cast matter. The judges may already be celebrities themselves, but the hosts of both *American Idol* and *Canadian Idol* have gained star status and become idols to millions of fans.

empathize: *share the feelings of someone else*

Young hopefuls try their best to impress the judges at *American Idol*.

HOW TO HANDLE STAGE FRIGHT!

- **Let the energy motivate you.** Those butterflies in your stomach produce a sense of anxiety, which gets you excited. Let this excitement motivate you and give you confidence.

- **Act it out.** Being on stage is like being an actor; you become someone else. If you see it this way, it may be easier and you might not feel silly.

- **Just relax.** This may sound obvious, but remember to BREATHE. Take nice, long breaths, as this will produce a feeling of calm.

- **Remember:** You cannot please everyone. Do your best and if your best is not good enough for some people, well then, that's life. Move forward and don't look back.

wrap up

1. In a small group, discuss the *Idol* show. Does everyone in the group like the show? Why or why not? Write down the reasons.

2. Imagine you are a judge in your country's *Idol* show. What would you look for in the winner? Explain why you would make a fair judge.

3. What advice would you give a friend who is auditioning for the *Idol* show? Would the Stage Fright tips be any help?

WEB CONNECTIONS

Use the Internet to research an *Idol* show in any one of the 20 countries that feature it. Write a paragraph to describe the show. Include information about the contestants, the host, the judges, and the latest winner.

CREATING A FIRST-HIT WONDER

Joel Parkes and his family watch Kimberley Locke perform his song on *American Idol*.

warm up

In a small group, discuss what it takes to be a songwriter.

By Ashante Infantry　　March 24, 2004

As a kid, Joel Parkes was obsessed with popular music.

"I used to fall asleep with the transistor radio and I thought the most important thing in the world was knowing what the No. 1 single was every week," recalled the Toronto-born singer/songwriter.

Well, this week it's Parkes who's topping a chart — at least his song is. "8th World Wonder," a tune Parkes penned with a pair of Nashville writers, debuted last week at No. 1 on *Billboard Magazine*'s Hot 100 singles sales chart.

The track is on the forthcoming album of Kimberley Locke, the Tennessee native who placed third on *American Idol* last season.

And Locke is slated to perform the heart-rending love song on tonight's episode of the wildly popular talent show. Parkes will be watching at home with his wife, two daughters, and assorted friends.

"Are you kidding?" he said between smiles and grins and unabashed laughter. "To write a song and have 30 million people listen to it live ... this is certainly a big moment in my career."

---

debuted: *first appeared*
slated: *scheduled*
unabashed: *not embarrassed*

He has studied journalism, criminology, and law, and worked as a carpenter, freelance magazine writer, taxi driver, and public defender.

In the summer of 2002, Parkes was in a Nashville studio with producer Shaun Shankel and writer Kyle Jacobs when he came up with the lyrics and melody for the chorus of "8th World Wonder."

*Seven days and seven nights of thunder
The waters rising and I'm slipping under
I think I fell in love with the 8th world wonder.*

Parkes is happy and he's going to be rich. He said his share from Locke's *American Idol* appearance tonight alone could net him as much as $20,000 if the show exercises its options for rebroadcast and website use. Imagine how many TV appearances Locke will make to promote the album, out in May.

"It means we're going to be secure," Parkes said somberly. "I can easily make a million bucks on this."

"But I'd like to own and run a record label. I want to be like Berry Gordy: find young talent and write songs and have 30 artists with No. 1 hits. That would be fantastic."

wrap up

1. Listen to the song "8th World Wonder" with a friend. Then write a short paragraph to explain the lyrics.

2. Create a chart to show five of your favorite songs. Include the headings: Song Title, Name of Artist, Name of Album, Favorite Lyrics, and Why I Like It.

OTHER HIT SONGWRITERS

Fefe Dobson (left) and **Chantal Kreviazuk** (below) are well-known singers and songwriters who also co-write with other famous stars — Dobson with Nelly Furtado and Kreviazuk with Avril Lavigne.

"If it looks good, you'll see it. If it sounds good, you'll hear it. If it's marketed right, you'll buy it. But … if it's real, you'll feel it."
— KID ROCK

"I sit down with a guitar player and if there's a situation I feel strongly about, or a guy that I've been thinking about or if I'm mad at a guy, it comes out."
— AVRIL LAVIGNE, on the inspiration behind her songs

"I have never tried to write this thing called a song that's played on radios all around the world, that window-cleaners hum, that people listen to in traffic jams. I was never interested in song: U2 came about through a sound."
— BONO OF U2, of his songwriting style (or the lack of it)

Written by ANNE BURKE Illustrated by NATALIE TWEEDIE

FYI

- Major recording label representatives often scout music competitions to search for new talent.

- The Barenaked Ladies started out as a group in high school. Their album *Stunt* reached #3 on the album charts in the summer of 1998 and sold more than 2 million copies in a couple of months.

wrap up

1. What happens when Matt, Daneisha, and the band jam together? Describe their musical differences.

2. Briefly explain how the DJ Crew discovers Daneisha.

3. Imagine you are the author of the story — select one frame and further develop a script conversation between the characters.

4. With a partner, plan a promotional campaign for a "Battle of the Bands" at your school.

HOW TO BECOME

warm up

Who is your favorite VJ? In a small group, share aspects of personality, style, and image that you admire.

CHECKPOINT

Watch a show on MTV and consider if you would become a VJ. Why or why not?

From the outside, it looks like being a video jockey, or VJ, is one of the best jobs in the world. You get to wear great clothes, interview rock stars, and hang around backstage at amazing concerts. Experience does not even seem necessary.

Of course, it isn't quite that easy. When music videos first went on-air in the late 1970s, they used radio disc jockeys to introduce the videos. The station managers quickly discovered that the skills needed in radio didn't really apply to live television.

MuchMusic and MTV make money by selling advertisements, not playing videos. VJs need to be able to keep viewers tuning in. They have to be informal, relaxed, and interesting enough to keep you watching when the music stops.

SARAH TAYLOR

These days, while some VJs have journalism experience, more are chosen for their unique ability to relate to viewers. No one at the video stations can say what this ability really is, but they know what it is when they see it.

"Everyone thinks it is about the looks," says producer Bob Pagrach, "but really, the VJs need to have a certain aura."

Rick Campanelli, Canada's most famous VJ, was studying for a Phys. Ed. degree when he got a summer job as a gofer at MuchMusic. Producers noticed his warm and engaging character, and began putting him on camera. Viewers took a liking to him, and soon he was the station's most popular personality.

Hannah Sung never planned to be a VJ at all, though she says, "If I had to

aura: *air or quality*
gofer: *assistant*

 FYI

Originally hired to introduce music video clips, video jockeys have become music journalists, interviewing major music celebrities and hosting their own television shows on the network.

Many VJs become famous and successful in their own right, like Carson Daly, JD (John) Roberts, and Sarah Taylor.

CHECKPOINT

As you read, select words or sentences to show that a VJ's job is much more than a dream job.

RICK CAMPANELLI

"Everyone thinks it is about the looks ... but really, the VJs need to have a certain aura."

CARSON DALY: FACTS

FULL NAME: Carson Jones Daly
PROFESSION: VJ
BIRTHDAY: June 22, 1973
HOMETOWN: Santa Monica, CA
EDUCATION: Loyola Marymount University
HEIGHT: 6' 2"   **WEIGHT**: 193 lbs.
CAREER START: KCMJ Radio

think up a better fantasy job, I would not be able to." She was a web designer who took a job at MuchMusic working at their online section. Her personality soon drew her to the onscreen side of the company.

Jennifer Hollett was working with puppets and waitressing in her native Montreal when a MuchMusic producer noticed her. Though she had little experience, she too shared with all the other VJs an extensive knowledge of music, the confidence to interview enormous celebrities, and the ability to talk to millions of viewers as though she was chatting with a friend.

"Just being able to think on your feet is really important," she advises aspiring VJs. "You have to react to whatever is going on around you and not be afraid."

Tony Young, better known as Master T in his VJ days, agrees that self-confidence is the key to a VJ career. But he also stresses education. "I'd suggest going to college or university and doing a communications course," he said. "If you can't wait two to three years, put together a demo-tape no longer than six minutes. Make sure it's shot well, you look presentable, and try to be as natural and comfortable as possible. And MAKE SURE YOU HAVE A PERSONALITY. Send it to MuchMusic or MTV and see what happens."

If you want to try this for yourself, MuchMusic and MTV occasionally hold open auditions across the country for aspiring VJs.

wrap up

1. What did MuchMusic and MTV station managers discover when they first used radio disc jockeys to introduce videos? Under the two headings — Radio Jockey and Video Jockey — write down a list of skills that are required for the job.

2. The author points out that VJs are chosen for a number of reasons. Identify the reasons MuchMusic personalities Rick Campanelli, Hannah Sung, Jennifer Hollett, and Tony Young were chosen.

3. Select one artist that has a video on MuchMusic or MTV and create a list of questions you would ask the recording artist if you were a VJ. In small groups, role-play the interview for your classmates.

Q: How does MuchMusic decide which music videos make it to air?

A. "We have a music committee made up of MuchMusic programmers and producers who meet and screen new videos all day. Then they decide who makes the cut. We judge videos on the quality of the song, quality of the video, as well as the song's airplay stats and the album's sales. We pick what's hot and pass on what's not." *(Craig Halket, Senior Music Programmer)*

WEB CONNECTIONS

Working with a partner, check out the origins of MuchMusic and MTV and trace their development and success. Write a short article that captures the popularity of the music video industry.

SOUND RECORDING

1877 Thomas Edison invented the cylinder phonograph, used to record and play back sound.

1887 Emile Berliner created the gramophone, a flat disk record player.

1906 The Victrola record player was introduced.

1925 The first electrically recorded discs, which standardized recording speeds, went on sale.

1931 The first LP (long-playing) records were sold to the public.

1946 Magnetic tape recorders, first introduced in the 1890s, came to the U.S. from Germany.

TECHNOLOGY

1964 The 8-track stereo tape cartridge was introduced.

1982 The first compact disc (CD) was marketed.

2001 MP3 players and MiniDisc hit the market.

2004 The iPod, weighing just 3.6 ounces, holds thousands of songs, and can last up to eight hours on a single battery charge.

wrap up

In a small group, discuss the following:
- When was the last time you listened to music on an LP record? A cassette tape?
- When was the first time you purchased a CD?
- MP3 players are beginning to replace stereos in many homes. Why do you think some people prefer MP3 players to stereos?

THE DOWN-LOW ON DOWNLOADING:

warm up

In a small group, discuss whether downloading is right or wrong.

Everyone has a different opinion on illegal downloading. Most people who download music files see nothing wrong with it. After all, they say, rock stars have lots of money. Other people think that it is as bad as shoplifting a CD from a store. Check out these opinions on downloading and decide for yourself.

Is it Really Free?

In a way, there really is no such thing as free music. Even if an artist posts their own songs on the Internet, they still had to spend time and money writing and recording. They need money to buy instruments, and to pay their bills while they write and rehearse. The money from CD sales helps keep them from going broke. If you download their songs from a pirate site, they won't have the money to keep making music.

It is no surprise that the big record companies fight piracy with lawsuits and even by arresting some fans. They see the free music movement as simple shoplifting. Many artists agree, even though they are reluctant to criticize their own fans — especially when CD and concert tickets keep getting more expensive. Still, artists should get paid for doing their job, and some of today's biggest stars have come down firmly against the downloading sites.

GIFT OR THEFT?

"If you can afford a computer, you can afford to pay $16 for my CD," says Eminem. The Barenaked Ladies are even more direct: "When the Gap went online, T-shirts didn't become free."

Many downloading fans argue that they are actually helping to promote the artist's work. Again, most artists see this as an excuse to get something for nothing.

"I suppose it should be a compliment that people dig your music so much that they're swapping it online. But thievery is thievery," argues R&B star Anastacia. "If you dig an artist that much, then you should want to keep that artist alive by purchasing the recording."

Some artists are not very concerned about whether or not their fans pay for their music. Says techno artist Moby, "Of course I support legal downloading, but, to be honest with you I'm pleased if someone downloads my music illegally. Again I feel quite flattered."

The New Wave: Pay to Play

Lately, some of the hype about downloading has switched to the growing craze for MP3 players and the leading online music seller, iTunes.com. MP3 players have created a cheap and easy way for fans to download music (many songs are under a dollar). Judging by the popularity of the very legal iTunes site, some of the free downloaders have decided to switch to a safer source of music.

wrap up

1. List what costs are incurred by the music artist when creating a CD.

2. The title of the article asks whether downloading is a "Gift" or "Theft". What do you think after reading the article? Discuss the issue in a small group.

Record Companies: HEROES or VILLAINS?

warm up

In a small group, discuss what you think the role of record companies should be.

Everyone knows that record companies sign up artists, record albums, and make videos for radio and TV stations. They promote and sell music, and make musicians rich and famous. Many people think of record companies as fairy godmothers who can turn an unknown into a "great, big star." Coldplay, Avril Lavigne, and Destiny's Child were all struggling musicians one day, and then in a flash they were flying around the world on private jets, playing concerts for thousands of people, and hearing their songs on every radio station in the world.

Another group of music fans think of music executives as villains who can ruin careers or make deals solely for their own advantage. What's more, they have taken action to halt Internet downloading and make it illegal!

Complaints Against Record Companies

- They are exaggerating the effects of downloading.
- They cannot do anything to stop downloading on the Internet.
- They should lower CD prices if they want to stop piracy.
- They are trying to slow down advances in technology.

Just Make Your Own CD

Do musicians still need to depend on record companies to promote and market their music? These days, some musicians choose to make their own record label. It doesn't take too much to make a music CD — just a name, a CD burner, and a color printer.

Homemade CDs can sell in big numbers. The example of the Barenaked Ladies is what every musician dreams about. The band's first album was a five-song cassette that sold over 100,000 copies in Canada alone. When they did sign with a major label, they had enough experience and influence to close a good deal for themselves.

More and more musicians are going with independent record companies. While they generally do not have a big budget, they do have more patience, energy, and dedication. They are able to give the musicians their full attention.

wrap up

1. Do you think record companies are fairy godmothers or villains? Discuss your opinion with a partner.

2. If you had to choose, which would you go with — a big record company or a small one? Why?

Before They Were ROCK STARS

warm up

As a group, discuss the personal dilemmas your favorite musician had to overcome before finding fame.

When you see them on TV or in videos, they seem to live a magical life. Some had amazing luck. But, surprisingly, many of today's biggest stars got to the top by the most old-fashioned route — hard work.

GREEN DAY

The members of Green Day come from a suburb of Berkeley, California. Their families were anything but well off: lead singer Billie Joe Armstrong's mother was a waitress, and bassist Mike Dirnt came from a broken home. The band grew out of a shared love of West Coast punk rock and a ferocious work ethic. Playing all-ages shows across the country, driving and sleeping in an old van, the band built up a huge following of like-minded kids. After a series of independent releases, they signed a major label deal, and started taking off on radio and MTV.

BIG BREAK An early afternoon appearance at Woodstock 94, when they were pelted with mud by the audience, became a media event, and cemented their punk reputation across the country.

50 CENT

Rapper 50 Cent broke sales records in 2003 when his first album became the best-selling debut album ever. If you had known Curtis Jackson a few years earlier, however, you would have been very surprised at this success. Born in Queens, New York City, 50 Cent had a difficult youth. Left without parents at a very young age, he was raised by his grandparents, and spent much of his youth on the streets involved in various crimes. By the time he was a teenager, he already had a lengthy police record. Fortunately for him, he also had a fierce intelligence, and knew that his talent for rhymes was worth more than a street rep.

BIG BREAK After a rough youth, 50 Cent met Jam Master Jay, an original member of RUN DMC. Jay took 50 Cent under his wing, and taught him the basics of song arranging and recording. 50 Cent used these skills to make demos that attracted the major labels.

EMINEM

Unlike many stars, Eminem has never made any secret of his difficult childhood. Eminem and his mother lived all over the States before they ended up in a poor neighborhood of Detroit. Em always had to work to support himself, and he married and had a child at a very young age. He earned his reputation rapping at talent contests and freestyle competitions similar to the ones in his movie *8 Mile*. His first few singles and EPs were ignored, but Eminem refused to give up.

BIG BREAK Eminem took second place in the 1997 Rap Olympics and afterward was approached by the head of a major record label who asked for his demo tape. The demo found its way into the hands of famed producer Dr. Dre — the rest is history.

FYI

When he first started performing, Eminem called himself M&M (which are the initials of his real name, Marshall Mathers). He later changed the spelling to Eminem.

GWEN STEFANI

With a rock star husband, good looks, and a successful solo career to go along with her band No Doubt, Gwen Stefani seems to be one of the luckiest people in the world. However, this was not always the case. Along with her brother Eric and their friend John Spence, Stefani started No Doubt in 1987 when they were still in high school. The band was starting to pick up steam when tragedy struck: Gwen's bandmate Spence took his own life. Despite this personal tragedy, the band soldiered on. Unfortunately, in the late 1980s, the music world was fixed on grunge and metal, and there was no place for a ska-pop band. No Doubt's first two albums bombed, and Gwen's brother Eric quit the band to become an animator. As if things could not get any worse, Tony Kamal, the band's bass player and Gwen's boyfriend of seven years, decided to break up with her. At the time, Gwen was still selling makeup at the mall, and it looked as if this would be her future. Instead, Gwen started writing new songs about coming to terms with the break-up.

BIG BREAK In October 1995, shortly after No Doubt recorded *Tragic Kingdom,* they performed the song "Just a Girl" at a California record store. Soon after the high-energy performance, local radio stations were flooded with requests for the song.

DO-IT-YOURSELF BANDS

DIY, or Do It Yourself, is the motto of countless bands across the nation. It means ignoring the conventional music business. DIY bands make their own records, print their own shirts, and book their own tours.

Coldplay financed their first album through part-time jobs, and were discovered playing in a Cuban café in Manchester, England. The Black Eyed Peas originated as a breakdancing troupe, and only started rapping to get more gigs.

wrap up

1. Select three artists and discuss, in a group, how the artists overcame personal challenges before becoming famous. What other types of challenges do you think rock artists face in today's world?

2. Imagine that your band has just had a "big break." In a paragraph explain how your band was discovered and the challenges you had to overcome to become famous.

WEB CONNECTIONS

Use the Internet to find out more about one of these artists. Create a collage of pictures, lyrics, and quotation that describes what his/her life was like before and after the big break.

Fan Mania!

They will follow stars home, write them letters of adoration, attempt to dress like them, cry uncontrollably, and spend their entire life impersonating them. Some fans will even go to the extent of plastic surgery to look like their idol. Whatever the means and whoever the star, there will always be a manic, lovestruck following.

warm up

What does the term "fan mania" mean to you?

1950s: Elvis Presley

Elvis was the "King" of rock 'n' roll. He thrilled his adoring fans with his new style of music and hip-shaking performances. Since his death, Elvis look-alikes and impersonators have become very popular. Millions of fans and tourists flock to "Graceland," Elvis' home in Memphis, every year.

1960s: The Beatles

The Beatles popularized "mop" hairdos and mod suits, and grew to become the most influential band of all time. They were greeted by adoring fans when they visited America in 1964. Fan hysteria known as "Beatlemania" swept through the US and the world. Female teenage fans screamed, cried, and fainted in their presence.

1970s: The Grateful Dead

In 1971, The Grateful Dead put a notice on their self-titled album asking fans to send them information about themselves. Fans were told to address their responses to: Dead Heads, P.O. Box 1065, San Rafael, California. From then on, intensely loyal Grateful Dead fans became known by that label. Some "Deadheads" even quit their jobs to follow the band around on tour for years.

1980s: Madonna

Madonna is one of the most successful artists in the history of popular music and is an idol to millions of people. Madonna keeps her fans intrigued by constantly changing her image and music. Her clothing styles set major fashion trends in the 1980s, and her looks are still copied today.

1990s: Nirvana

Nirvana kicked off the early 1990s grunge style. Despite the death of Kurt Cobain, the band's singer and guitarist, in 1994, their music is still very popular today. Nirvana's grunge style combines punk and heavy metal with pop melodies. Their rough clothes and anti-fashion stance have become the style of a new generation of followers.

2000s: Britney Spears

Originally known for her girl-next-door image, Britney Spears has become known as a pop vixen. The Britney craze has even led girls to try plastic surgery to look more like their idol. Her wild style, from belly shirts to body piercing, and slick pop sound are widely imitated.

Fan Deaths

- The December 3, 1979 Who concert is considered the most horrific concert tragedy in the US. Eleven fans were crushed to death and dozens more were injured after a mob of people surged toward the stage.

- On June 30, 2000 at a Pearl Jam concert in Roskilde, Denmark, nine people were killed after being crushed and trampled by a mob of fans.

- In January of 2001, at a Limp Bizkit concert in Sydney, Australia with 50,000-60,000 other fans, a 15-year-old died after being caught in a crowd surge while she stood in the mosh pit.

In a 2002 concert in Sheffield Arena, England, fans of rock idol Gareth Gates broke the records with their screaming. They reached 130 decibels, even louder than the fans of the Beatles in the 1960s. The sound is almost as loud as standing 40 feet away from a supersonic jet!

A US survey in 2001 reveals that among adult rock fans, 84% are more likely than average to engage in extreme sports (bungee jumping, sky surfing), 47% are more likely to own a motorcycle, and 12% are more likely to own a personal watercraft or powerboat. They are also 53% more likely than average to play a team sport (softball, soccer). The study also shows that rock fans have distinct purchasing preferences and create great opportunities for advertisers.

wrap up

1. List the words and phrases used by the author to describe fan mania.

2. With a partner, discuss whether the actions and behaviors of the fans are a good or bad thing. Write a paragraph to explain your point of view.

Guitar Dreams

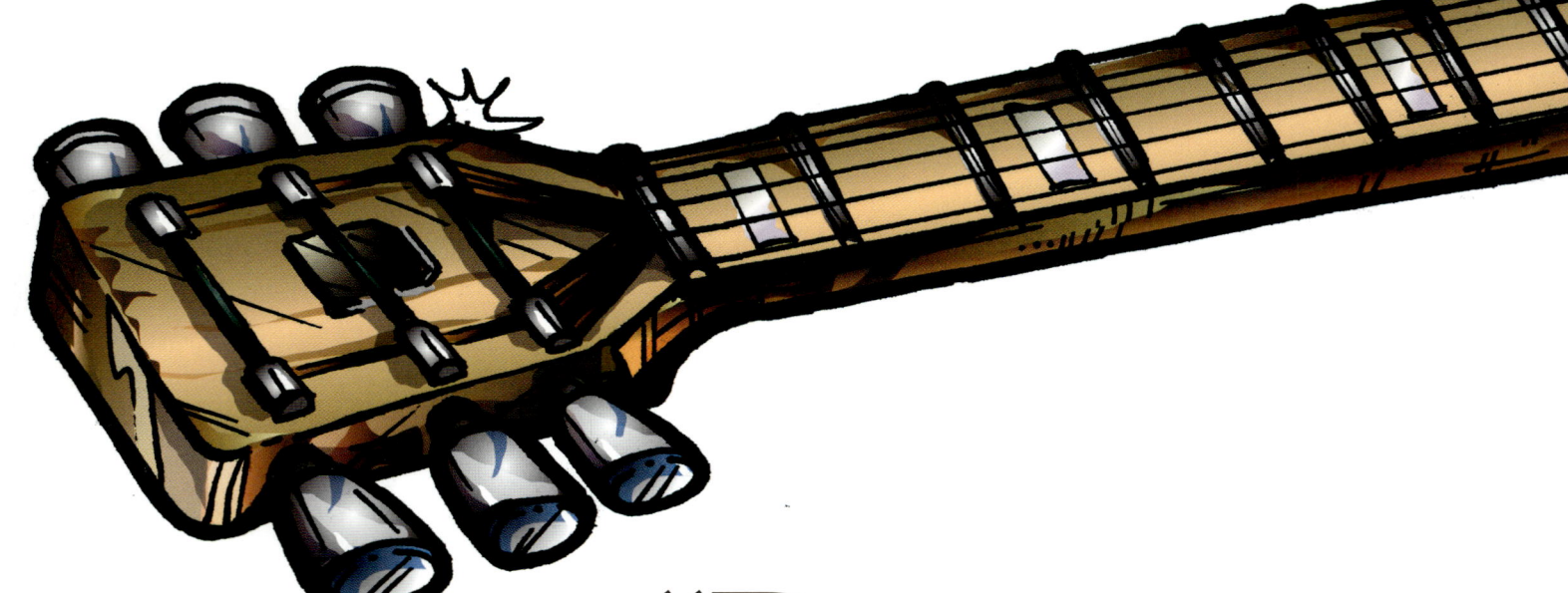

warm up

Has anyone in the class ever met a famous rock artist or movie star? If yes, share the experience.

"Dude, you're crazy."

Nathan finished his sandwich, and threw it in the garbage.

"I don't care, Jimmy." He tried to sound confident. "It's worth a try. The guitar my uncle gave me is worth a lot of money. I checked it out on the web."

Jimmy looked disgusted. "Man, if it's so valuable, why would you sell it?"

"I'll never be any good. I've been practicing for weeks and I'm getting nowhere," Nathan explained, as they headed back to class. "Look," he continued. "It's simple. A guitar signed by a big star like Johnny Revolution doubles in value. There was one last week on eBay.

"If I can get JR's autograph on it, I'll have enough for a half-decent car when I get my license next month. His band is playing at the arena tonight. It'll be my only chance."

"Well, it's your guitar," said Jimmy, shaking his head. "But I still think you're nuts. You'll never get backstage. You're just going to end up wasting your time hanging around the arena door."

Nathan knew his friend was probably right, but he could not stop thinking about how cool he would look with a new set of wheels. As they sat down, he leaned over toward Jimmy's desk.

"We'll see who's wasting time when you're walking to school next month, and I'm cruising along in my new wheels." Nathan always had to have the last word.

By seven o'clock that night, Nathan was starting to regret his bravado. The bus ride downtown had taken forever. The first band had already started playing when he got to the arena. He didn't have a concert ticket and every door at the arena was locked. Finally, he found the backstage entrance, but an enormous man stood guard in front of it. His T-shirt even had a big danger sign printed on it. Nathan swallowed, and built up his courage.

---

bravado: *a false display of courage*

"Excuse me, sir; I was wondering if I could go backstage to get my guitar signed by Johnny Revolution?"

Slowly the guard looked down at him. His voice seemed to come from his toes.

"No."

Nathan was not going to give up that easily.

"You see, I'm saving for a car, and if I get this guitar signed, I can …"

A huge finger jabbed his chest. It felt as hard as a piece of iron.

"I said, NO!"

"Right then, you're finally here! I've been waiting for you to show up. Come on; we've only got a few minutes!"

Nathan and the security guard were equally surprised by the interruption. The voice with a heavy British accent came from a slim woman dressed in black leather. She brushed aside the security guard and grabbed Nathan's arm, pulling him backstage. Nathan tried to look around, but he had to run to keep up with the woman, the heavy guitar case banging his knees.

"Hi, I'm Terri — I left you that message earlier," said the woman as she dragged him along. "We've phoned every music store in town to find that guitar! The guy at Music

Town said you might make the show, but he wasn't sure."

Nathan tried to tell Terri he didn't know what she was talking about, but she barely took a breath as she guided him through stacks of sound equipment.

"We couldn't believe it when we opened the guitar cases today and found all three of Johnny's 1972 Galaxy guitars had broken necks. I mean, what are the chances?" she laughed. "And he cannot go onstage without one. I had no idea they were so rare! I called every guitarist in town to find you."

Finally, Nathan managed to interrupt her. "Listen, Terri — I'm not from the music store."

"*What?*" She stopped, horrified. "Then what were you doing out there with that guitar case?"

Embarrassed, Nathan blurted out the truth.

"I was hoping to get my guitar signed by Johnny Revolution so I could sell it on eBay and buy a new car."

"Why me? Why me?" Terri moaned, leaning on a skyscraper of black cases. "Please, please tell me — what kind of guitar do you have in there?"

"Well, it's a 1972 Galaxy. Everyone knows Johnny loves them, that's why I thought he might sign …"

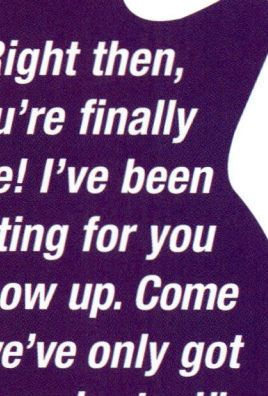

"Right then, you're finally here! I've been waiting for you to show up. Come on; we've only got a few minutes!"

"I don't care who you are. Come on, we need that guitar!"

Terri was now running, her boot taps echoing on the concrete floor. They went up a set of dark stairs, and squeezed into what looked like a miniature guitar store.

"Smokey! Here's the guitar."

Grinning, the bearded roadie took the case.

"Whew! That was close. The band is just about to go on," he said.

With lightning speed, Smokey changed all the strings on the guitar and ran onstage with it.

Terri pushed Nathan out of the alcove.

"Here, kid — you can watch the show from here."

Nathan found himself right next to the stage. For a second, he caught a glimpse of the thousands of screaming fans. Then the lights went down. There was a deafening explosion, and the band ran onstage. Nathan could hardly believe his eyes — Johnny Revolution was playing his guitar!

The show was a blur. Nathan tried to watch and remember everything, but it all went by too fast. All too soon, the band was playing their last encore. With another huge fiery explosion, they left the stage.

As the exhausted crowd filed out, the stage was filled with roadies packing up all the equipment. Nathan looked around for Smokey, but he couldn't find him in all the confusion. Finally, tired of being told to get out of the way, he wandered into the arena hallway. No one could tell him where to find his guitar. He checked his watch and realized he would miss the last bus. He was angry with himself.

"Great!" he muttered. "I came for an autograph and have lost my guitar!"

Feeling defeated and stupid, Nathan leaned against the wall. Down the corridor, he could hear a familiar accent. It was Terri asking the backstage crew if they had seen him.

"Hey kid! We've been looking for you! Come here. I want you to meet someone."

Standing next to her was a thin man soaked in sweat. He wore a heavy bathrobe. Under his arm was Nathan's guitar case. He stepped forward and shook Nathan's hand.

"Hi, I'm John," he said in a hoarse voice.

"I know." Nathan was thunderstruck. It was his hero, Johnny Revolution himself.

The rock star laughed.

"I want to thank you for saving the show. This is a beautiful guitar."

He handed Nathan the case.

"Uh, I was hoping you would sign it," said Nathan.

"Already done," Johnny smiled. Frowning slightly, he went on, "My road manager Terri said you were going to sell it?"

Nathan suddenly felt a little guilty. "Yeah, I wanted the money for a car," he replied.

The rock star nodded.

"I understand, kid. I rode lots of buses when I was your age. But let me tell you something. When I was your age, I had the cheapest guitar in the world. It sounded awful, it hurt my fingers, and I broke a million strings. Still, I really believed I could be a great guitarist. My family didn't have much money, but my Dad worked two jobs to buy me my first Galaxy. I still play it every single night."

"I've tried to play … and I practice, but I'm not any good," explained Nathan.

"Listen, kid. No one is any good in the beginning," his new friend laughed. "But it's a lot easier to learn when you have a great instrument like this one here. You might be better than you think. Anyway, it's up to you. I just want to say thanks again for letting me play it."

Nathan was already eating his lunch when Jimmy sat down at the table the next day.

"Hey dude, did you pick out that car yet?" Jimmy joked. "You must have felt stupid hanging around that arena all night, right?"

"Actually," said Nathan, talking around a huge bite of sandwich, "I did get it signed."

Jimmy's mouth fell open in surprise.

"No way! Did you put it up on eBay yet?"

"Nah. I decided I can wait for a car."

"Well, then what are you going to do with it?" asked Jimmy.

Nathan smiled. "You know what? I think I'm going to keep practicing for a while yet. An expert said I had some real potential!" Jimmy looked at him, confused. "What?"

Nathan just laughed in reply. No one would believe the truth anyway. Humming the chorus of the latest Johnny Revolution hit, he threw his lunch bag away and headed back to class.

wrap up

1. What is the message in this story? With a partner, discuss how the author uses each of the characters to help convey this message.

2. What events that led Nathan to change his mind about selling his guitar?

3. Imagine Nathan is a grandfather. He is giving his guitar to a teenage grandchild. Write a short note from Nathan explaining why the guitar is so special.

ACKNOWLEDGMENTS

The publisher gratefully acknowledges permission to reprint copyright material in this book.

Every reasonable effort has been made to trace the owners of copyrighted material and to make due acknowledgment. Any errors or omissions drawn to our attention will be gladly rectified in future editions.

Gordon Downie: "Toboggan Hill" from *Coke Machine Glow*.

Ashante Infantry: "Creating a First-hit Wonder," from *Toronto Star* (March 24, 2004). Reprinted with permission of Toronto Syndicate Services.

Jewel: "Pretty" from *A Night Without Armor: Poems by Jewel Kilcher*. Copyright © 1998 Jewel Kilcher.

Tracey Stefanucci: "Teaching Teens the 'Value of Music'" from *YOU think Magazine* (Summer 2003, v5, n10).

Fender Telecaster and Stratocaster: Registered trademarks of Fender Musical Instruments Corporation.

Fender Stratocaster and Fender Telecaster: Copyright © 2005 Fender Musical Instruments Corporation. All rights reserved.

iPod: Copyright © 2005 Apple Computer, Inc. All rights reserved.